CENTERED in CHRIST

I can do all things through Christ

who strengthens me.

Dr. Annette West

Centered in Christ

Printed in the United States of America

Copyright 2020 by Annette West

LCCN: 2020920632

ISBN: 978-1-7320260-0-1

by *JATNE* Publishing

Editor: Yolanda Whitehead

Book cover: Tiana L. Whitehead

Spiritual -- Christian -- Daily Living -- Bible Study

Teaching Source –Empowerment

DEDICATION

Special thank you and my deepest appreciation to the beautiful authors that shared with us in this book. I thank the Lord that they are examples in action that exemplify His truth in their lives. Thank God for their willingness to share from their experiences to empower others.

I honor and thank Anna J. Roseboro for sharing her poetic work with us. May the Lord continue to enrich her as she continues to inspire us and share with the world.

How to Use This Book

This book has several powerful devotionals and activities. The devotions are ideal for daily use, and for group discussion or Bible study. Prior to beginning the book, take the time to pray to the Lord to reveal what He would have you get from this anthology.

- *Read* each devotion.
- *Say* the affirmation out loud. Go back to it throughout the day.
- *Pray* the prayer after each devotional, make it personal.
- *Answer* each question.
- *Reflect* on the devotion. Write the key points and your thoughts.
- *Read* the poems in the poetry section. Reflect on how they speak to you.
- *Create* your own poem in the poetry section by responding to each line.

- *Meet* our authors. You will find a biography of each contributor.

- *Study* the Scriptures for Further Study list.

Table of Contents

Introduction

Christ Must Become the *Essence* of Who You Are.

To the believer, Jesus Christ is to be the center of everything. Jesus clarified that authentic life is found in Him and Him alone. When embracing Christ, the believer learns to commit to Him and depend on Him. Often, people get caught up in doctrine, theology, and tradition. However, a Christ centered life is one in which each person develops a personal relationship with Him-recognizing that He is the source of life and living.

The Christ centered life, Christocentric, Theocentric, life involves the whole of the Christian, mind-body-spirit. It is the revelation that Jesus Christ is the very center of everything. Everything revolves around

Christ, focuses on Him, testifies about Him, and points to Him.

We must be gospel centered. Jesus showed that all of Scripture is about His redemptive work, and that life eternal is to know the only true God. Even the Apostle Paul regarded the gospel as the first importance for the believer.

The gospel, the good news, is how God conveys His benefits to His people. Including forgiveness of sins and the absence of shame and guilt. Christ wants us to become immersed in the wonder-working power of God. He wants us to take the time to learn and develop characteristics that align with Christ Jesus' example.

We have the New Testament to remind us that when we become saved, there is the expectation of how to live daily—keeping Christ Jesus first in our lives—embracing His fullness in the Father, Son, Holy Spirit. This way of living also includes loving Him with our whole being and loving others as we love ourselves.

Through time, I have learned the importance of living a life centered in Christ. He is the single influence that has had the most significant impact on this earth. I believe each person's life will change as they commit to shifting their ways, thoughts, and desires to be more connected to Him. They will have a *daily motivation for growth in Him* and His ways.

The believer learns that Christ Jesus is the only way. Pure joy comes in looking and dealing with reality and seeing Christ as the one that helps us through each day. This joy comes from experiencing a relationship in Him. As committed followers of Christ, we center our lives on Him. He is the one we look to for direction, and we consistently desire to spend more time with Him. We commit to obey His commands. Thus, the primary aim of a Christ centered life is to *glorify, exalt, and worship God in spirit and in truth*. Our lives echo Paul's words,

That I may know him, and the power of his
resurrection, and the fellowship of his
sufferings, being made conformable until his
death. (Philippians 3:10)

We need to understand how the gospel of Christ equips us to deal with the vast issues that arise in life. God has a predestined plan for each of us. Understanding His purpose helps us grow and develop to be more like Him.

In this book, nine powerful women connect to share how they learned to have a centered life in Christ. They will share their hearts and experiences to help us see that it is possible to *live an intentional life loving and serving Christ.* The wisdom shared presents God's plan for His daughters and His grace that empowers and equips us to live a life in His reality, His ways, and His ideals. Scripture declares:

For if these things be in you, and
abound, they make you that ye shall neither

be barren nor unfruitful in the knowledge of

our Lord Jesus Christ. (2 Peter 1:8)

As you journey through this book, the hope is that you will come to understand who you are in Christ Jesus through:

1. **Devotions.** The devotions will share thoughts and insights to empower the reader towards becoming centered and committed to living a life that exemplifies the Lord.
2. **Scriptures.** The scriptures will help the reader see God's view of their life.
3. **Direction.** The practical tools shared will provide the reader with proper direction and perspective to understand what is right in His sight for spiritual health.
4. **Christ.** The combination of devotions, scriptures, and direction will together help the reader see that everything they require exists in their relationship with Christ.

In this effort towards a *Centered Life*, the Bible is clear that regardless of what is going on, we must come to Him for the needed rest to find the strength to move forward in Him. He can keep us and deliver us so we can be free in Him.

> *Come unto me, all ye that labour and are heavy laden, and I will give you rest. Take my yoke upon you, and learn of me; for I am meek and lowly in heart: and ye shall find rest unto your souls. For my yoke is easy, and my burden is light.* (Matthew 11: 28-30)

Living Life with Purpose

Before I formed thee in the belly I knew thee;

and before thou camest forth out of the womb

I sanctified thee, and I ordained thee

a prophet unto the nations.

(Jeremiah 1:5)

Even before we were in our mother's womb, God had a plan for us. When He created us, His expected end is that we prosper. We will never feel complete until we discover that purpose. Not only find it, but pursue it. In our lives, we must ask ourselves who or *what are we living for and what is our purpose.*

Some people go through life just existing and never finding their real purpose. They go through life with no sense of direction and cannot thrive. Some never think about what they want to accomplish in life—just taking life as it comes.

Life has many challenges, but we can *navigate* it to reach our *destiny* if we have a sense of *direction*. Without a plan, we live life carelessly and full of trials and errors. It has been my experience that whatever I live for becomes my passion or drive.

When living outside of Christ, I lived for myself and what made me happy. I never thought about God who created me. I moved through life for the moment, with no standards, and never planned or strategized my next move.

Being a very adventurous young lady sent me down a dark road and I hid this from my family. I was eager to try new things that were not always good for me, never thinking of the consequences. Not knowing my worth and value, people took advantage of me and I allowed it. When a person has no standard, they are subject to do and accept anything.

Deciding to give my life to Christ was the best thing for me. My *life* now has a *purpose. Joy* came over me when I truly *repented and accepted Jesus Christ* as my Savior. Christ has now become the focus in my life. His desires became my desires, and His passion became my passion. Thus, navigating through life became easier. *Why?* Because *Christ* now becomes *the leader*, and me, I have become the follower.

After letting go of my will for my life and accepting Christ's will, He showed me my purpose. The Holy Spirit taught me all things about my life and how to live. I now know my *value* and *purpose*. My life is full of *joy* and *peace*.

Do tragedies or calamities hit my home? Yes, but I no longer have to turn to alcohol or a man to console me. Now, I turn to the Anointed One. He has given me the road map to victory.

We each can learn to commune with Him and find peace and the comfort we need. It could come through a song, a sermon, a prayer, reading the scriptures, or just quiet time with Him.

The Lord, through His Holy Spirit, has a way of calming the storms in our lives. Placing Him as a top priority in our life gives us the advantage above our adversaries. When there is danger, the Holy Spirit will send out an alert, DANGER! DANGER! DANGER! This warning will allow us the opportunity to turn and go in another direction.

With Jesus as our True Shepherd, before we venture into anything, we must check with Him and see if our plans line up with His will for our life. Sometimes we can move out of season and timing with God. Sheep know the voice of the shepherd. We must learn the voice of our Shepherd, Jesus Christ, we will obey Him. I say all the time, "partial obedience is total disobedience."

The COVID-19 pandemic of 2020 has proven that it takes more than just a Sunday morning service to have a relationship with Christ; this is a daily walk. A constant reminder, we are not our own; we are bought with a price; that price was the blood of Jesus. It is going to take denying the flesh. I'm not just talking about turning our plate down. But when those ungodly words want to come out, we must have enough self-control to hold it. When God says go right, and we want to go left, we must deny what we feel to do what He says.

Sometimes I want to do what I desire. However, when I think of what I would lose in Christ, my *reward* outweighs my flesh's desires. Through many unnecessary trials and errors, I have learned how to *transform successfully*, to living a life centered in Christ.

Sebrina Blanding-Johnson

I will check with Him to make sure I align with His plans for my life.

Prayer Time

Heavenly Father, thank You for forgiving me of my sins. It is with a grateful heart that I worship You. You have been a strength when I needed power, peace when I needed peace, and a hiding place when I needed rescuing. As I continue to follow the purpose You have created me for, help me not to become weary and lose focus. Let me always remember that You are the one in control. When I become anxious, please remind me that in You, I have a hiding place. Although family and friends may forsake me, You, Lord, will never leave me. It is in Your wonderful name, I pray, Amen.

Questions to Ponder

Have you discovered your God-given purpose? If so, how are you going about fulfilling that purpose?

_____

_____

_____

What is it that brings you satisfaction and fulfillment even on your worst day, and what about it brings you fulfillment?

_____

_____

_____

What would you do for a living even if you didn't get paid for it, and why?

_____

_____

_____

What part of your life gives back to the Kingdom of God? Describe it.

_____

_____

_____

Reflection:

_____

_____

_____

_____

_____

_____

_____

_____

_____

_____

_____

_____

_____

_____

_____

_____

_____

The Waves

Fear thou not; for I am with thee: be not dismayed; for I am thy God: I will strengthen thee; yea, I will help thee; yea, I will uphold thee with the right hand of my righteousness.

(Isaiah 41:10)

As a little girl, my dad would always take us to South Padre Island, Texas, for our summer vacation. My mom and dad were divorced, but they had a great friendship, and he always asked my mom to come with us. We didn't all stay in the same room, but He wanted our vacations to seem as normal as possible.

Looking back now, I am so glad my parents got along after their divorce. It made it easier for us kids. The beach has always been my happy place. As a kid, I loved getting in the water and riding on my boogie board, diving into the waves. But the *sucker punch waves,* the ones that knock you off your feet when you least expect it, I did not like those at all!

I know we have all had something very hard and life-changing happen in our lives. Those moments seem to come as *waves* and *knock us down.* When the waves come, some may stay within the tide of defeat until finally getting the strength to crawl up and out. But what happens when the *waves of life* continue to knock us down repeatedly?

One of those life-altering moments was when my mother passed away suddenly at the young age of

55. She went to a hospital on Sunday, and the next Sunday, I sat devastated as I watched her take her last breath. The doctors initially thought she had a terrible case of an upper respiratory infection and pneumonia. A week after she passed, we would find out she had B-Cell Non-Hodgkin's Lymphoma, and no one had any idea.

Shortly after my mom's passing, my then 14-year-old daughter was diagnosed with a brain tumor and had a 6-hour brain surgery for a biopsy. The doctors told us that the tumor was inoperable and recommended six weeks of radiation. My daughter got to ring the bell upon completion of radiation, which was one of those *riding the waves* moments!

But every three months, we feel *the waves of fear* as she goes in for MRI's to check on the tumor that has taken up residency in her brain. The past two MRI's have shown that the tumor is shrinking, and we praise Him for the good news. These two life-changing moments with my mother and daughter happened in a matter of two months.

We *pray and praise* because we know God is there, but I would be lying if I didn't say that the waves of fear creep in so easily. They try to take over and discourage us from living the life we still have to live. They try to keep us hostage and forget that this life is so precious, even with the challenging situations we have gone through and will continue to go through. The enemy will do that! He will use those waves to his advantage, but we cannot allow him to do so.

Some waves are so much stronger than others. The ones that come out of nowhere are the hardest to face. You don't expect the wave to come so abruptly and set you back, knock you down, or put you flat on your face. From experience, I can say that *God is always near during those struggles,* the bad news, and the life-changing moments. He knows the waves, and He knows you. It is hard sometimes to understand that when we are confronting a wave. We find ourselves riding, crashing into, and sometimes knocked over. It is part of life, and although we would rather it not be the case, these waves test our faith.

Those are the times our prayers seem to get few and far between. Those are the times we can only see our pain. We try to muster any of the strength we have left, but we grow tired.

To *conquer the waves*, keep *pushing through*, keep *praying*, keep *seeking God*, and, most importantly, *keep living* your life. The enemy would like for us to stop in our tracks, to stay vulnerable, to cower in fear, but God says, "My power works best in weakness!" He wants you to come to Him. He wants you to call out His Name. He wants to help you through the troubled water of life, to see that there is hope and life at the top of the wave. This hope and life lives through our testimonies.

Testimonies are so vital because they are your story. No one else's; you get to share the raw, vulnerable, and painful times with others, and then you get to follow that with your story of redemption, restoration, and courage. We all have that. We all can reflect on a time in our life when God showed up.

Sometimes we have to glance back and lock at the wave that knocked us down and see how far we have come! It not only motivates us on, but it spurs on others. Our walk with Christ is so essential for *making it through the harsh waves,* and our relationship with Him is what keeps us moving on into the life we are called to live!

K'Cee Lee

The waves may crash Into me, but I will survive in You Lord.

Prayer Time

Dear Lord, I pray that as the waves of life come, You remind me that You are my strength. Allow me to focus not just on what is happening at the moment, but where this wave may take me. Allow me to see the bigger picture; to see the plan. Guide me as I push through the tough waves and know that through my weakness, You are strong! Amen.

Questions to Ponder

What is one of the most difficult "waves" you have had to conquer in your life?

_____

_____

_____

How did you make it through? If you are still in the wave, what are you doing to help make it over or through the wave?

_____

_____

_____

What is a wave you have conquered that you can see God's hand in as you look back?

_____

_____

_____

Reflection:

_____

_____

_____

_____

_____

_____

_____

_____

_____

_____

_____

_____

_____

_____

_____

_____

_____

Sheltered Soul

The Lord is my rock, and my fortress, and my deliverer; my God, my strength, in whom I will trust; my buckler, and the horn of my salvation, and my high tower.

(Psalm 18:2)

My soul was not always sheltered in the Lord. Reflecting on my life experiences, I realize that I did not always understand that Christ was my shelter. I thought of my church, the place I went to on Sunday, my Pastor, as my support and protection in my life. At a point in my journey, I pondered what the term shelter means to me.

The definition of shelter, according to Dictionary.com, is something beneath, behind, or within which a person, animal, or thing *is protected from storms*, missiles, adverse conditions, a refuge. For example, when hazardous storms occur, the sky may darken, the winds may blow, the rains fall, and a person takes shelter for protection to avoid the harsh conditions.

Looking back over my life, I can recall when a storm of defeat and shame hit me during my divorce. The fracture of my family rocked my world. When I said, "I Do," I thought it was going to be forever. I never imagined my marriage *wouldn't* work.

However, I found myself in a severe life storm. A place where my finances changed as we divided assets. It was tough in this season and I wasn't trusting in God to protect me during this time. I had to leave my condo and move into an apartment. I had to protect my boys and ensure we were out of harm's way. I had to budget my finances because my income changed, moving from a two-income household to a single-income household. I had to adjust expenses according to my single monthly income. There wasn't an opportunity to depend on anyone else but myself. I felt the divorce stripped me of my normal life and I did not trust God anymore!

What I saw and endured didn't reflect what I now believe regarding God being my shelter in my marriage. During this storm, trust issues surfaced. I felt as if those I trusted, God and my spouse, failed me. *I cried out to the Lord* to *help* me in *my unbelief!* I couldn't see clearly; I felt like I was stumbling through life, and it took much time to refocus.

As time passed, I remembered my past experiences of success. God reminded me He had come through for me before and He would continue as I called on Him. Thus, I *gave it all to God*, not trying to figure it out on my own.

In this season, I was still angry and hurt and realized I needed freedom from the hurt in my heart. I couldn't do it on my own. My hands seemed to make a mess of things. When I thought about Christ, in my eyes He was too busy to engage with my questions and issues. Maybe He had other problems or concerns above mine He needed to address. There had to be more challenging situations to ponder, such as world peace or medical treatments with new cures to engage. He didn't have time to give me a solution, or so I thought.

I eventually *refocused on the Lord*, stopping to take time to breathe and rethink my behaviors. I called upon the Lord in prayer and found that my Creator desired to help me, all while He was also helping others. He was concerned about my healing from my past relationships and partnerships.

I was still recovering from the wounds of misunderstandings and lack of confidence in knowing my worth. Yet, I realized that Christ was listening and desired to hear me share what I was going through with Him. I admitted to Him that the divorce was a rough storm, and I was struggling with forgiveness. What I thought to be small and not a priority *was important* to Christ, and only He could help me through my problems to find healing. He could provide a solution.

Thus, I forgave my ex-husband and myself, which allowed me to *align my walk with God*. I thanked the Lord for reminding me to *surrender* to Christ and *forgive*. If I wanted Him to forgive me, I must forgive my ex-husband. That forgiveness was a critical key to victory within my life. I'm not saying it was easy, but it became doable as I daily talked with the Lord and took time to get into the scriptures and refocus my thoughts, and much prayer.

Consider our lives. *Storms will come and can hinder us.* We may feel unprotected, uprooted, ungrounded, or unstable within our life's journey. It is our shelter in Christ that provides confidence in our position of certainty in Him.

Jesus Christ, *our shelter*, has been talked about for nearly 2000 years. Since the creation of the world, He has commissioned us to follow His guide and understand our uniqueness to live an abundant life. We are not to be swayed with life's challenges, but *steadfastly rooted and grounded in love*. We should replicate His living through our lives.

Storms, deceitful voices, broken relationships and insecure mindsets occur in our lives. Our shelter is not stable if these things easily blow us over. The deceitful behaviors become patterns in our life and begin to affect others. With everything going a person may not even realize what they are displaying to others.

For the believer, one's shelter must be the firm witness of Scripture rooted and grounded in prayerful devotion. Walking and relying on the Word of God will provide *wisdom and understanding.*

The Lord will order our steps, unlock treasures, and ensure victory and confidence.

When a person is firmly sheltered in faith, they are well-positioned, rooted, and grounded to guide with confidence and inform the world of *God's glory.* Thus, when I learned that Christ is my shelter, I became positioned to guide and advise those I encountered to share His amazing glory. Sharing God's glory from a sheltered place is what *He calls all of us* to do. I am so much stronger having gone through this storm.

Lekeisha Mosley

I will stay sheltered in Christ as I know He will keep me through the storms of life.

Prayer Time

Heavenly Father, I come before You boldly with confidence today. As I walk in this journey of life, I know You will shelter me during the storms of life. I will continue to refocus and recharge in You on the truth that I am more than a conqueror in Christ. I am led by the Spirit and not through the challenges that may come before me. I have learned to take life's challenges and learn from them. I am commissioned to walk in forgiveness and focus forward and continue to live in the shelter Christ provides. I will continue to remember that I am well-positioned, rooted, and grounded to guide with confidence and inform the world of God's glory. I will continue to be a light and advise those I encounter with my story. Amen.

Questions to Ponder

What does sheltered mean to you?

_____

_____

_____

Think about a time when the Lord was not your shelter. What negative characteristics did you display in that season of your life?

_____

_____

_____

How do you think God feels when you do not allow Him to shelter you?

_____

_____

_____

When Christ is your shelter, how is your walk and life different from before?

_____

_____

_____

Reflection:

_____

_____

_____

_____

_____

_____

_____

_____

_____

_____

_____

_____

_____

_____

_____

_____

Be Intentional with Christ

And he said unto them, *"Come ye yourselves apart into a desert place, and rest a while."*

(Mark 6:31)

Anyone who has had any lasting relationship will tell you, "it takes work!" This is true for a marriage, friendship, or a relationship with a family member. We must be intentional about not only maintaining but also growing the relationship. In a marriage, this may be a scheduled date night. With a friendship, perhaps it is a regularly scheduled girls' day. For a family member, we may set aside time to catch up with a telephone call. *We intentionally make room for what and who is important* in our lives.

A few years ago, I went through a grim period in my life. The void and pain inside of me were deep. The spark that caused this void was the separation from my husband. However, if I am honest, the split was just the tip of the iceberg. I realized that I was a very broken person who had learned to present myself to the outside world packaged up nicely behind a pretty mask.

From the outside, nobody would ever know the internal struggles I was experiencing. My broken marriage resulted from many things. Two contributing factors were that I genuinely did not know who I was and did not know my value.

As the void grew more profound, I attempted to fill the space. I made sure that I was always busy. My schedule was jam-packed with volunteering at my children's school, volunteering at church, working, shuffling kids back and forth to activities, and many outings with friends. I rarely spent time at home, avoided being alone, and hated any silence. Around the same time, our women's group at church was diving into a new study that came along with a challenge—*commit* to journaling, praying, and spending quiet time with the Lord for 40 days straight.

I vividly recall the feeling I had as I held the new journal in my hand and thought about what was happening in my life. The Lord spoke to me. He presented two options to me that night. The first option was to continue to put a Band-Aid over the hole in my life. Sure, it feels right at the time because I am avoiding the issues, but eventually, I would crumble. The Band-Aid of busyness and avoidance would not heal me. The second option was simple. *Choose God!* Therefore, I did.

For the next 40 days, I woke up early every morning and began my day with scripture, prayer, and journaling. I was *intentional* about this time with the Lord. As it became my number one priority, I learned to meditate on God's word. I appreciated the silence as I opened up my heart to the one true healer. As I did, the Lord not only answered my prayers, but He began showing me who I was, who He created me to be. Not only was I *intentional with spending time with the Lord,* but our Father was so very intentional about spending time with me!

In Mark 6:31, Jesus instructs the Disciples to come with Him to a *quiet place* and get some rest. We must understand that the Lord is our comforter. We experience much-needed *rest in the arms of Christ.* If we are intentional about getting alone with Him regularly, He will fill the void in our lives. However, when we attempt to fill the void with worldly things, we become so busy that we cannot hear our Lord amid all the outside noise. If we wish to experience all that He has for us, we have to make time for Him. We must *be intentional about reading His word* and learning what He has to say about our lives and us.

If you read further on in Mark 6, after Jesus instructs the Disciples to come alone with Him, you notice that the next event that occurred was the feeding of five thousand with just five loaves of bread and two fish. Notice that the miracle happens *after* Jesus tells the Disciples to come alone with Him for rest. If we wish to witness God move in our lives, we must go alone with Him to a quiet place.

My 40-day challenge has now turned into a three-year *intentional relationship* with our Lord and Savior. After making quiet time with Him a priority and after resting in His arms, I have experienced many blessings and personal miracles in my life. One of which is the Lord restored my marriage. I give all praise and honor to Him for this, but more importantly the void in my life no longer exists. Christ has sealed the hole. *That* is the genuine *miracle* that occurred after I committed to an intentional relationship with Christ. I now know God created me for a *purpose*, I know my *value* and I walk in my purpose with *confidence*. Even if my separation from my husband ended in divorce, I would still have a testimony to share. He made me whole! Christ is the center of my life and I will always remain intentional in my relationship with Him!

Yolanda Whitehead

Lord, I will be intentional in my relationship with you!

Prayer Time

Dear Heavenly Father, I thank You for always being intentional with me. Lord, the relationship that I have with You is the most important relationship in my life. Therefore, I know that I must make time and room for You before I look to anything or anyone else to fill any void I may experience. Today, I commit to spending time with You daily. I want to get to know more about You and what You say about me and my life. I will be intentional in living a Christ centered Life. Amen!

Questions to Ponder

Have you ever placed a person or thing as a priority over Jesus Christ in your life?

_____

_____

_____

How do you think it makes Christ feel when you don't have Him as your priority each day?

_____

_____

_____

How do you feel about quiet time? Do you incorporate it into your schedule?

_____

_____

_____

What is one practical commitment that you can make today towards being intentional about your relationship with the Lord (designated prayer time, waking up early, journaling, etc.)?

_____

_____

_____

Reflection:

_____

_____

_____

_____

_____

_____

_____

_____

_____

_____

_____

_____

_____

_____

_____

_____

_____

Living in The Core of His Will

I am crucified with Christ; nevertheless I live; yet not I, but Christ liveth in me; and the life which I now live in the flesh I live by the faith of the Son of God, who loved me, and gave himself for me.

(Galatians 2:20)

I remember the first time I realized that the only way for me to live is to no longer do anything in and of myself. This way of living is a process that many will have to grow in and develop how God intended. What do I mean when I say no longer do anything of myself? I mean that I had to be God-conscious in my decisions, responses, and behaviors.

I'm not saying this is a simple process, but we must make a conscious choice each day to choose righteousness rather than just going with the world's flow. If you look up the word *core*, you will find that it means the central or most important part of something. Living in the center of God takes courage.

Looking back over my life, I see a trend related to the outcomes of things I do of my own free will, bad choices. The results not only affected me, but they trickled down into the lives of my children in such a way that it would bring disappointments, unnecessary hurt, and pain. These results were due to my inability to make conscious decisions. It not only affected my present situation, but it also affected the future.

When I think about learning to allow God to lead, I remember the scripture in Amos 3:3 where it asks a question - Can two walk together, except they be agreed? At first, I thought that was only concerning husband and wife, but it relates to various aspects of this walk with Christ. So, I pondered on that a minute. I realized God himself was saying to me, how can we become as one without us coming into agreement with each other to accomplish my will for your Life?

Consider this, unless you believe with your heart and the actions align with your behavior, there is no way you are living in the Core of His Will for your life. To live in the Core of His Will, I had to deny myself to the point of death. In 1 Corinthians 15:31, Paul says, "I protest by your rejoicing which I have in Christ Jesus our Lord, I die daily." You may ask, how is this possible? How can we die daily? It means that whatever I desired to do had to be measured by righteousness, and what God expected of me had to be more highly than what my flesh may have tried to persuade me to do.

God's will is that we have an expected end as described in Jeremiah 29:11, it says: "For I know the thoughts that I think toward you, saith the Lord, thoughts of peace, and not of evil, to give you an expected end." Too often, we enter places God never intended for us to be, and we end up in chaos and confusion. So I may be made a more perfect sacrifice, I had to deny myself of those things that would lead me astray.

Often, we are in the midst of the development and miss the mark because we are not mature enough to handle the situations we find ourselves in. We are free-will agents, capable of making our own decisions, needing to take full responsibility for what those decisions may be, or what they may cost us.

Ultimately, God knows what we will do or what we will say before we think it. He has orchestrated our lives according to His design. God purposefully puts things in place for us to learn and grow. We choose and decide the what, when, how, and why of our very own lives.

When you think about how He moves, you understand that God is all-knowing, and living a Christ centered life is good for our health. It is a life of choosing to live for Him by deciding to pursue peace and not comfort. I've learned that there is no peace in being comfortable.

When we operate outside of God's grace, we prioritize fitting in over living in the perfection of who He is. God is a God of peace, and everything centered in the Core of who He is also displays peace, trust, and stability.

Once I could see how my decisions were causing me to miss the mark, I applied the principles of God's word to my life and in my decisions. Things changed for me, and I had a sense of fulfillment in obeying God's word. What I got through those experiences drew me to align my thoughts to what the word said, and it allowed me to see futuristically what would transpire if I didn't apply the word.

I also realized that no matter how I changed my thought process and behavior, what was already in the works had to come to fruition. What I had done in the past had a time clock on it, in how it affected my children. Now they must learn how to make good choices for their lives and their children's lives. We don't realize how it could trickle down. We do all we can to cause a turnaround, but the choice is theirs, we just have to let God do what He will in their lives.

Not doing what God wanted me to do, it cost me, but it was worth it. I did not say why or woe is me. I believe I had to experience it to position myself in a place I never thought I could dream to be, getting to the next level in my purpose. I am no longer fighting for peace, but fighting in a place of peace. I am no longer fighting for truth, but I am grounded in His truth.

I'm so thankful for all the experiences and opportunities that God allowed me to face. Living out God's plan from the center of His will positioned me for God's best, and not anything less. If He can do it for me, He will do it for you.

Living in the Core of God is where you find joy. Psalms 16:11 says: *"thou will show me the path of life: in thy presence is fullness of joy; at thy right hand there is pleasures forevermore."*

Jacqueline Smith

Oh, Lord I will dwell in Your Presence!

Prayer Time

Father, I thank You for giving me the perfect sacrifice and the example of how to live in the center of Who You are. Teach me to consider You in all I do. Help me align my thoughts with your thoughts, and put my desires in the *core* of your perfect will ,so I can fulfill your purpose for my life. Lord, help me live out what You teach me daily. Breathe in me a newness of life and cause me to be fruitful in all I do. I will continue to yield myself unto You and apply the truth of who You are in every area of my life. I thank You Father God for your grace, mercy and compassion toward me, I pray in the mighty name of Jesus Amen.

Questions to Ponder

What does having Jesus as your core mean to you?

_____

_____

_____

Think about a time when your decisions caused
unnecessary hurt and pain. What characteristics did
you display in that season of your life?

_____

_____

_____

How do you think God feels when you do
something out of His Will?

_____

_____

_____

Do you notice a difference when you consider God
in your decisions? What difference do you notice in
your daily efforts?

_____

_____

_____

Reflection:

_____

_____

_____

_____

_____

_____

_____

_____

_____

_____

_____

_____

_____

_____

_____

_____

Anchored Soul

Which hope we have as an anchor of the soul, both sure and stedfast, and which entereth into that within the veil; Whither the forerunner is for us entered, even Jesus, made an high priest for ever after the order of Melchisedec.

(Hebrews 6:19-20)

Oh, my goodness, when the storm is coming your way, what do you do? You hopefully realize that life has its trials and tribulations.

When I was growing up, if you heard noises outside in my neighborhood, it was the children running around or hanging out, sitting on the curb, but even that didn't get too loud. However, when there was a block party, oh yes, it was a good time.

As I look back over my life, I can recall that it was not always a peaceful place within my home. The noise often got so loud, my head hurt. Then I went to school and heard cruel words from children because my clothes and shoes did not measure up to theirs. Well, my mom had six kids and mouths to feed. Thus, I dealt with many cruel people and turmoil all around me. I lived in a dangerous and unpredictable world, yet it didn't destroy me.

It is funny that amid all of this mess, I was thinking about Jesus. I can recall my yearning, my words to Him, not knowing that He was the *anchor* that kept me sane.

I say this because I did not go to what they call *the church*. I did not go into a physical building to hear a person in the pulpit talk about Jesus since I left my Grammie and Big Pop's house in the country when I was six years old. There was, however, a Bible in the house, and I would open it and read.

When I graduated from high school and moved forward, I still yearned for Christ. I sought a church and started attending, even gave my life to Christ. There was lots of teaching that came forth on how to quote scriptures. I learned how to teach a Bible class—hearing about the Bible, lots of stories about the page's characters. However, I never heard about being rooted, firmly *postured, grounded, centered*, and *anchored* in Jesus. The foundation was there, but it was incomplete because *I had yet to become anchored* in Christ.

In ancient times, the anchor was a symbol that represented safety; thus, Christians adopted the anchor as a symbol of hope. If we think about it, the anchor has excellent benefits to a ship as it holds it in place. It represents *strength* and *security*, keeping the vessel from drifting because of wind and weather shifting.

Consider our lives. We can easily get tossed *back and forth* when not *postured, grounded, centered, and anchored* correctly in the Lord. It is having an anchor in Christ that fixes our position of certainty in Him.

Since the creation of the world, God has existed. His people manifest His invisible qualities. Jesus said He is unique, and the believer must emulate Him. Thus, as His follower, each person must seek daily to walk in His uniqueness. Replicate His living through their life. Develop a personal relationship with Him, our *anchor.*

Think about it, part of one's Christian witness is how they help *guide* people to *safety, security,* and *salvation* in Christ. When one gets tossed about with the winds of doctrine, trickery, and deceitful scheming, it should become clear that the landing to our faithful anchors have broken. Like a buoy adrift, a Christian is no longer doing any good for Christ and may endanger others without realizing the peril they have created.

The Lord promised that all the descendants of Abraham experience a blessing. We want the blessings of health, wealth, and prosperity, but those things are fleeting. Instead, we receive every spiritual blessing in Christ, the *hope, anchor* of *our souls.*

For the Christian, one's anchor must be the firm witness of Scripture grounded in faithful and prayerful devotion. It is not enough to read the Bible; we must also study and develop a relationship with Christ. This practice requires faithfulness, being intentional to our daily walk in Christ. Committed to reaching the profound and beautiful depths that the Lord has predestined for us.

As we grow and become *anchored* in Christ, we should realize that hardships come. Yet, we must be careful not to allow ourselves to drift from the anchor. We must stay connected to the *Power Source Jesus Christ.*

I thank Christ that during the confusion and turmoil in my young life, He was my anchor when I didn't know it. He gave me the strength to hold on to life. After being saved, I eventually learned to have a relationship with Him. I learned to commit to a relationship, trusting Him for all things, knowing that my anchor is in Him.

When a person becomes firmly anchored in faith, they are then well-positioned to guide and inform the world of God's glory. Thus, when I learned to anchor myself firmly in faith, I became positioned to guide and advise those I encountered and share God's glory, what God calls us to do. That is to be:

"The visible manifestation of

His invisible presence."

Annette West

Daily I will strive to stay rooted and grounded in the Lord.

Prayer Time

Lord, there are so many storms I encounter in life. Some are tougher and rougher than others. People that I encounter may be unkind and inconsiderate. There may be times when it seems the mountain is too high to climb. The valley is too deep to wade through. While the wind and rains may be so hard in the ship, it seems no end in sight. The sky too dark to see clearly. There may be crying and frustrations. There can be a feeling of being ready to burst from the heart. Yet through it all, being anchored in Your arms means that I can weather it. I am stronger than I can image in You. You are my strength and shield. You are my hope in all things and at all times. As I build a daily relationship with You, I am assured and reassured at others that You King Jesus are forever with me. I am blessed to be in your warmth, having my soul anchored in You. Thank You, Lord, for being so great to me. Amen.

Questions to Ponder

Define what anchored in the Christ means?

_____

_____

_____

Think about a time when the Lord was not your
anchor. What characteristics did you display in that
season of your life?

_____

_____

_____

How do you think God feels when you are not

anchored in Him?

_____

_____

_____

When you are anchored how is your walk and life

different from before?

_____

_____

_____

Reflection:

_____

_____

_____

_____

_____

_____

_____

_____

_____

_____

_____

_____

_____

_____

_____

_____

_____

Leaning on the Lord

Trust in the Lord with all thine heart; and lean not unto thine own understanding. In all thy ways acknowledge him, and he shall direct thy paths.

(Proverbs 3:5-6)

Maya Angelou said, "When people show you who they are, believe them." Unfortunately, I did not hear this until later in my life. People had shown me who they were, but I always wanted to see the best in others. There was a time when I put too much trust in people close to me, only to allow these same people to break my heart. Yet, there came a time when I had to take the blinders off; and my, it hurt! During the pain and anguish of knowing I had given so much of myself, I realized I was *leaning* in the wrong direction.

I had become a creature of habit with my beliefs. Over the last ten years, I learned that *leaning is* an *action* word; I cannot say that I am leaning on God and then turn around and do the total opposite of what I am relying on God for. Leaning solely on the Lord did not come easily by any means. I had to take a long, hard look at how I depended heavily on certain people and not seeing myself as valuable without them. The sad thing is, I did not realize I did that until I found myself all alone.

Suddenly, I wondered what just happened. Many things ran through my head. Why did I not see things unfolding? Why me? Was I too trusting on all sides? I did not get an answer; all I could say was wow, I did not see that coming. Nothing happened overnight. I did not forgive right away; I did not trust anyone for many years. I shut myself off from everyone, including God. But do you not know *you cannot hide from His presence?*

No matter how hard I tried to shut myself off, there was always that one constant in my life, and His name is Jesus. He loves me so much that He would not allow me to become lost in my pain. Instead, I felt pressed on every side; He would not let me fall. Even though I was torn inside and could not find the words to say to Him or open my Bible, He was still there.

When I leaned in the wrong direction, the one scripture that played in my spirit was Proverbs 3: 5-6. Until finally, I heard God saying, "Why are you trying to figure things out that I have already straightened out for you?" Not until then did I take a long look at myself and the years I had wasted, *lost in my private pity party.*

I make masks during this current pandemic for people. Just consider that I cannot trust that the needle is strong enough to hold the thread without breaking to make these masks. I will frequently stop and check the needle instead of leaning on the fact that I use good quality material.

When I reflect on my situation, it was a tragedy for me. At the beginning of my tragedy, it overwhelmed me. One day my husband was home with me, life was good, and the next day he was incarcerated. I went from a two-person income to one. I had to deal with the embarrassment of people knowing and watching as they whispered at my workplace. I had to be strong for my children; I had to hear from my children how this made them feel. You can image that as a parent it angered me for my children to go through this tragedy, and it made me angrier. As a woman I can handle the wind when it blows hard my way, but I could not handle seeing my children being *tossed to and fro.* I hurt, I was angry; I wanted to scream and beat my fists into something or someone, but did I? No, however, I still failed the test in showing strength in my relationship with Christ.

As life was dealing me some hard blows and I was reeling from the shock, I took my eyes off Jesus. He was waiting to take my burden upon Him, but instead of giving it to Him, I wallowed in self-pity far too long.

Often, we think we know what is best for us, but if we truly knew, we would keep our focus on the only One that provides us with inner peace and joy no matter what we are going through. I know first-hand, as *I lost my joy, hope, peace, focus on Him and in my life.*

My Lord is the only One that truly knows me. Jeremiah 29:11 says, "For I know the thoughts that I think toward you, saith the Lord, thoughts of peace and not of evil, to give you an expected end." This was the scripture I spoke to myself. I *leaned* on the Lord because I remembered He had greater plans for me. He loves me *so much* that He wants the best for me.

After all that I endured in that long season of despair, I know with a *full assurance,* that though I might bend, I will not break as long as I am *grounded, rooted,* and *leaning* on The Father and not my own understanding, which I did for far too long. Thank God He does not count it against me and sees me through the blood of His Son, *washed and renewed.*

Now more than ever, I know that every day may not be what I want it to be, but the one thing I know is that I am leaning and trusting in the Lord no matter what comes my way, for I know from where my help comes. So let me encourage you, don't give up on yourself; always trust that the One who shed His blood for you is right there with you, just waiting for you to lean on and trust in Him. Jesus said He "would never leave nor forsake you," so believe Him.

Tuesday Payne

I will stand firm in my faith, as I lean on the Lord.

Prayer Time

My Father and My God, thank You for allowing me to lean on You. I count it a privilege and an honor that You know my name; therefore, my goal is to follow the path You have predestined for me. I know now that as long as I stay focused, rooted, and trusting in You, I will not fall into any trap that the enemy tries to set for me. I also want to thank You Father God, for not allowing me to break, even when I was leaning in the wrong direction. Thank You for allowing the Holy Spirit to prick my heart that it might reconcile me back with You. That is Love. Amen.

Questions to Ponder

What are your strengths' and weaknesses? If you are unsure, pray to the Lord to reveal them to you.

Strenghts'_____

Weaknesses_____

Once you receive your answer from the Lord, will you allow Him to work powerfully in you during good times, but mostly through weakness?

_____

_____

_____

What are some practical things you do if you realize you are leaning in the wrong direction?

_____

_____

_____

What will you do to stay focused on the plan you believe God has for you?

_____

_____

_____

Reflection:

_____

_____

_____

_____

_____

_____

_____

_____

_____

_____

_____

_____

_____

_____

_____

_____

_____

_____

_____

God's Peace and Security

Behold, I will bring it health and cure, and I will cure them, and will reveal unto them the abundance of peace and truth.

(Jeremiah 33:6)

God's *peace and security* are instrumental in all believers' lives. His Love is the essence of everything for us. It is He who created us and keeps us safe daily as He covers and protects us amid life's disappointments.

Yet, I did not know or understand this when I was going through the shame and embarrassment associated with a divorce. For me, it was the worst thing that could have happened. It brought a wave of emotions that transformed my love into hatred. I was ostracized by those who blamed me when they did not know my story. At that moment, I questioned God, but He was silent.

As I reflect on those years, I see that God had a work for me to do. I became an advisor to abused women, a conference speaker, a suicide intervention team member, and went back to school. As I threw all my pain and energy into helping others, I did not know that *God was healing and preparing me* for a greater ministry. God had me so focused on working with others through their hurt that I did not have time to deal with my brokenness.

With all that was going on, I believe God's silence was His way of healing me of my heartaches and disappointments and letting me know that I could learn to *live in peace after the storm*. I had reacted by not reacting to others and pretending that this was just a nightmare that I would eventually wake up from. Even though I tried hiding my genuine feelings from others, I could not hide them from myself or God. All I needed was to hear my ex say he was sorry.

In time, God allowed me to minister to a woman who was going through what I had experienced. As I prayed for her, the Lord showed me I was just like her. We were both broken but not shattered. As I continued to pray for her, I felt *a peace* that I had never experienced. God released the brokenness that I had hidden within. As I sobbed, God revealed to me I was no longer bound by my shame.

As the tears flowed, I felt a *renewed peace* as His presence comforted and restored me. At that moment, I surrendered every part of me and cried out: *"I forgive me Lord and I forgive him too."* I believe if I had not said these words, I would not be here today.

From that confession, the Lord gave me a new vision to take my mind off myself and bless somebody else. The vision was simple and serves as a daily reminder that it is time to grow up and stop trying to do things my way and *learn to do what God commands.* A testimony of hope and a living witness to others that God can deliver and heal.

Deliverance and healing can only occur when we take ourselves out of the equation and allow God's peace and security to *take root* in our life and learn to forgive others that have wronged us. When I forgave myself God's Love restored my peace and showed me how beautifully unique I am. The Lord also reminded me He created me for greater and life's situations would mature me. It was then that I realized that trials will happen, but they serve a purpose. These trials are designed to challenge and prepare me to become a living testimony to others.

His Love and compassion for us are evident as He continues to shower us with blessings that *protect* us physically, *restore* us mentally, and *redirect* us daily. He continually forgives us when we do wrong and break the commandments. He does not leave us alone but steps in when we cry out and repent by wiping our slate clean as often as we call out with a sincere heart. He forgives, chastises, and restores our broken hearts, as He delivers us from the mental and physical infirmities meant to destroy us. For it is God's peace and security found in Jeremiah 22:6, that heals those exposed to the dangers associated with doing things their way.

Therefore, it is imperative that we repent of our sin. Then, the *power of forgiveness will transform us.* This shows others that God's *peace and security* has changed and redirected us.

No longer are you consumed with hurt, pity, and anger. Instead, all negativity is replaced with love, kindness, compassion, hope, and peace because the Father has looked beyond your faults and believes in you. Therefore, as you walk on your journey and become *"Christ Centered"* keep your eyes on Him and not on the world. For He is a good, kind and compassionate Father who patiently waits to heal and restore when we falter on life's journey.

Robin Whitehead-Rudolph

I never want to be hurt, but I know it is always a good day to be healed.

Prayer Time

Heavenly Father, I prepare myself to be a living testimony of Your divine will. Thank You for daily blessing me by renewing my compassion, hope, and love in You. While strengthening my heart and mind with Your healing virtue to mature me in my faith. You always bless me with your grace and mercy when I endure life's pain, suffering and heartaches. Lord, I thank You for the struggles in my life that will help me walk in integrity and obedience, that will result in my having an awesome testimony that says: "God's Peace and Security are the reasons I have survived life's Storms." Amen, Amen, Amen.

Questions to Ponder

Describe how it feels to be at peace within yourself after you have been through a storm. Are you currently at peace?

_____

_____

_____

How secure do you feel when the hard issues of life arise?

_____

_____

_____

How do you feel when you trusted God, and see how He covered and protected you in your breakthrough?

_____

_____

_____

Is there someone God is calling you to bless/help? If you're unsure, take time to pray about it.

_____

_____

_____

Reflection:

_____

_____

_____

_____

_____

_____

_____

_____

_____

_____

_____

_____

_____

_____

_____

_____

Anna's Poetry

Modeling a Model Who Models Christ

Being centered in Christ is more than a notion
It takes years for roots to grow and branches
to bear fruit.   Some of us learn how important it is
by reflecting on the models who taught us to trust
in the Word of God to guide our lives.
The model and teaching of my maternal
grandmother, Jamar Elena Williams, are the
parentheses for two key events. One began when I
was a pre-teen and the other occurred when I
became a mother, and later lost my son,
Robert A. Roseboro.
The poems show the varied ways that being
centered in Christ can strengthen us and
His Spirit can comfort us.

The Heart Tree

There is a tree in my heart
      Was it there at the start
Of my life as a wife and a mother
Through the cares and woes
      And the joy that just goes
Along when one lives with another?

The trunk is my past
    The part that will last
When the children have come and gone.
    They are the branches -
    Reaching out, taking chances
Outside in the world and the throng.

This tree in my heart
I hope is a part
Of all I have known and still love.
It's trite, but it's true,
      But, the growth's due to you
Who grounded me in God's love above.

Anna J. Roseboro, August 1993

Fist Fights Won't Do It

She had quite a temper, that Anna's
Classmates and teachers couldn't stand
When she got angry, she'd swing and hit ya
Big or small, short or tall, she'd just swing 'round
and hit ya

"Do not fight. It is not right.
Just turn the other cheek!"
"But Gramma, they'll tease me.
I don't want to look meek."

"It's not right to fight. You can run away!
Meekness is strength under control," she'd say.
"Run away from a fight. I'll look like a fool!
Running from a fight is not cool at school!"

"Control yourself. It's more pleasing
Even if they keep on teasing."

"But Grammama I have got to fight.
Every day they tease and taunt me
Saying I'm black, but I talk so white!"

So I fought and was caught and expelled from
school
The day before graduation.

Depressed, in total desperation, saw I'd not been
cool.
Fighting that guy created a total mess
I cried, looking in the mirror in my new dress.

I'd failed to stand up and failed to be strong.
Grammama was right all along
It was not right to fight with fists.
I fought with my fists and look what I missed.

Turn the other cheek; it's okay to be meek.
Meekness is strength under control.
You'll have more peace within your soul.
You'll stand out in the throng as strong.
Yes, Gramma was right all along.

Anna J. Small Roseboro, 2019

Grammama

Grammama was a powerful woman
Devoted to family and to God,
Best known for what she taught:
Walking the walk,
      not just talking the talk.

Devoted to family and to God,
Grammama got us to church weekly,
Walking the walk,
      not just talking the talk,
Grammama taught us
      to love by the Bible.

Grammama got us to church weekly
      to sing those hymns
         and hear the Word.
Grammama taught us
      to love by the Bible.
She loved it so much,
      she disciplined by it.
Grammama taught us
      to love by the Bible.

Best known for what she taught;
Walking the walk,
not just talking the talk.
Grammama was a powerful woman.

VISITS

Military men had come,
with news no parent expects to hear.
"Ma'am, yesterday in Sasebo, Japan,
Navy officers found your son in his apartment…

 dead.

"He didn't show up to the ship.
They went to his apartment.
They found him...

dead."

"My son is dead?
He's never coming home!"

My son is dead!

In the twilight, I reel in limbo
In that haunting ground
Between dread of awake
and terror of nightmare.

Tension tightens my neck
Flows down my back
Becoming a fiery fist
at the base of my spine.
Fingers clutch the fragrant bed sheet.
Thighs stiffen into planks

And toes tingle like ice cubes.

That night…I lay in bed
praying to process the news.

(An image appears…)

A doorway opens…
I recognize the place.
Bright light streams around two figures.
I recognize the people.

Standing there is Grampoppa,
Haloed by light
Light streaming all around
Extending his hand in welcome.
"Come on in, son!" he says.

Behind him, is Grammamma,
Peaking over his shoulder.
Light streaming all around
Her welcome smiles from her eyes.
"Come on in, son!" he beckons.

The voice is familiar. I'd heard it over the years.
Grampoppa said that when the uncles come home
for Mother's Day Dinner.
 "Come on in, son!"
He said it at Father's Day and birthday gatherings.
"Come on in, son!"

Grampoppa and Grammama are there to greet my
son!
To welcome him home with them
In heaven.
I believe it.

Heaven is home.
So, I'm content.
I sigh and breathe.
I believe it.
All is well.

Bob is with Grampoppa.
Bob is with Grammama,
All is well.

I sense another voice,
"Anna, my child. Your son, Bob, is home.
And see, he's Home with family.

Ah, at last. Now at peace.
        Ah, at last. Not a peep.
                I drift into healing,
comforting sleep.

Written by Anna J. Small Roseboro, August, 2006

Wonder Woman

Wonder Woman
Showed up
Spoke up
Loved, cared
And shared

Dignified
Seldom cried
In public
But alone
Sometimes on
The phone

Balanced pride
With humility
The Bible
Was her
Guide

Teaching
By doing
Modeling
Integrity

Demanding
Honesty
Living
The truth

Showing possibilities
Encouraging risk
Reminding us

Not to
Fight with
Our fists

Wonder Woman
Was Grammama

Wonder if
I can
Be
Like her.

Showing up
Speaking up
Loving, caring
And sharing.

By Anna J. Small Roseboro, January 2020

Drafting a Poem about Life

Centered in Christ

Reflect on the devotions you have read. Which is one that speaks to you? Write four lines that summarize your experience reading and reflecting on that devotion.

(1) _____

(2) _____

(3) _____

(4) _____

Repeat lines 2 and 4, then add lines 5 and 6 to expand ideas introduced in lines 2 and 4.

(2) _____

(5) _____

(4) _____

(6) _____

Repeat lines 5 and 6, then add lines 7 and 8 to expand ideas mentioned in lines five and six.

(5) _____

(7) _____

(6) _____

(8) _____

Finally, repeat lines 1, 3, 7 and 8 in this order:

(7) _____

(3) _____

(8) _____

(1) _____

Now, reread and revise as needed. What words, phrases, or punctuation need to be changed to make your poem flow? Now you can share in an email or blog post.

* See "Grammama" on p. 99

Meet the
Centered in Christ Authors

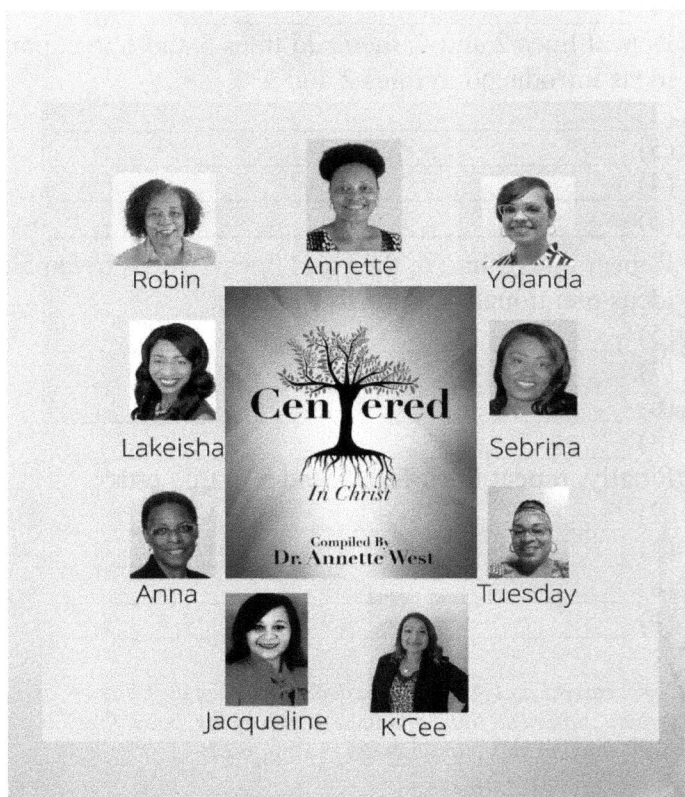

Sebrina Blanding-Johnson

Prophetess Johnson was born and raised in Brooklyn, NY where she met her husband and married in 1988. She gave her life to God in 1992, ordained a Deaconess in 1994, an Elder and House Prophet in 1999.

She and her husband moved to South Carolina in 2002, where she founded a Non-Profit (501c3) Organization, Woman to Woman Ministries in 2004. Prophetess Johnson also has a young woman's mentoring program named His Jewels (ages 12-21). She is the Leading Lady of Holy Temple of Jesus Christ in Summerton, SC where her husband is the Overseer. Early this year she accepted the mantle of a Prophet, and is the House Prophet of Holy Temple of Jesus Christ under the leadership of her husband, Overseer Raymond Johnson Jr.

She has (3) adult children, (1) son-in-law (4) grandchildren. She is a graduate of Saint Leo University where she obtained her B.A. in Business Management and Human Resource Management.

She is the author of <u>Broken into Purpose</u>, a Certified Life Coach (Transitioning Coach), and is the manager of Sumter Psychiatry Assoc. in Sumter, SC. Besides her full-time employment, she owns a S & N Services, a medical billing organization. She enjoys journaling, spending quiet time with her husband, and helping to transform women into positive, productive members of their community. Her greatest joy is being a servant of the Lord Jesus Christ.

Prophetess Johnson's favorite scripture is (Psalms 119:105)

Thy word is a lamp unto my feet, and a light unto my path.

Email: womantowomanministries16@yahoo.com

K'Cee Lee

K'Cee Lee is a native of Texas. She is married to her high school sweetheart, Jonathan, of 18 years and is a mother to two: her son Dominik and her daughter Ashlynn. They now reside in SC, where they planted roots after her husband completed his time in the Navy.

She was a Navy wife for almost ten years and served alongside her husband in youth ministry for six years. Besides being a full-time wife and mother, she has worked for the US Air Force for 13 years. The military is near and dear to her heart as her husband, sister, sister-in-law, and brother are veterans.

K'Cee coaches small group leaders at her home church, Freedom Church in Moncks Corner, SC. She also hosts a small group for women in her home. She has mentored young women in their walk with Christ during her time serving in youth ministry and continues to use her time to serve in the women's ministry. K'Cee has a passion for writing and helping women of all ages. She has always loved to write, and it started as a young girl; she would write mini books to share with her family. Now she shares her writings on a different platform.

One of her favorite scriptures is, (Exodus 14:14)

***The LORD shall fight for you, and ye shall
hold your peace.***

Check out her blog out at www.kceeleeblog.wordpress.com

Lekeisha Mosley

Lekeisha Mosley is a highly successful Business Identity Strategist and the owner of MyIdentityDrivenLife, LLC. Lekeisha, is a certified coach, speaker, and teacher through the John C. Maxwell Team.

She has impressive achievements in administration, counseling, and business management throughout her professional career with the United States Government, which has provided her with opportunities to impact the global market. She has received acknowledgments and appreciation for her achievements by assisting her clients living on purpose and intentionally in their relationships personally and professionally.

Lekeisha is committed to saving lives as a Court-Appointed Special Advocate for abused and neglected children worldwide. Lekeisha has received her bachelor's degree in Business Management and her master's degree in Management and Leadership. She has also served her country for 12 years and became an honorably discharged veteran in the United States Army and Air force.

Lekeisha is using everything she has learned as an opportunity to speak and influence others across the world and to be an advocate of change to her clients and community. She is happily married to her husband, Charles Mosley II, and has two awesome boys: Dewayne Jr, Myles, and Charles III.

Current Accomplishments:
Work for Positive Power Christian Media, LLC
Job Title (Co-Producer and TV Host of The Lekeisha Mosley Show) Radio Host and TV HOST of The Lekeisha Mosley Show

Mental Illness Advocate bringing awareness of healing and informational resources for others who need assistance.

Author of two published books:
- How to Get Unstuck: Jumpstart your Life in Your Relationships
- Free Yourself: Breaking Free to Enjoy your Journey of Love, Success, and Wellbeing

One of her favorite scriptures is, (Isaiah 58:11)

And the Lord shall guide thee continually, and satisfy thy soul in drought, and make fat thy bones: and thou shalt be like a watered garden, and like a spring of water, whose waters fail not.

Tuesday Payne

Tuesday Payne has the heart to serve. She is the fourth of six children, a mother to two and grandmother (Nana) to five beautiful grandchildren, to which she devotes most of her time. Tuesday is a firm believer that children should be trained to develop into the best of themselves with God as their guiding light and always trust and lean on Him.

Tuesday has studied many courses attaining a BA in Psychology and a MA in Human Services. Although these are crowning achievements in her life, she is never more satisfied than when she attends to the elderly's needs. She has the heart to serve. Money and accolades don't move her, but a deep inner spirit connection in knowing she is helping others does. She now gives much of her time to advocating for voters, believing that all humanity has certain rights that must not be taken for granted or from anyone.

One of her favorite scriptures is, (Proverbs 3: 5-6)

Trust in the LORD with all thine heart;
and lean not unto thine own understanding.
In all thy ways acknowledge him,
and he shall direct thy paths.

Anna J. Small Roseboro

Anna is a wife and mother, poet and coach, and National Board Certified Teacher with over forth years of experience. She has taught English and Speech to students in middle school, high school, college, in public, parochial, and private schools in five states. She now is directing her attention to online ministries, coaching new writers and mentoring early career classroom teachers in middle schools, high schools and colleges.

In the various states where she's lived, Anna fellowshipped with Bible-believing and teaching congregations. Her services have varied from praise and worship leader, choir director, Sunday school teacher, to director of summer vacation Bible schools. She is most excited about what she is learning working with youth teaching that praise dance, singing and pantomimes are Bible ways to minister. What a blessing!

Recent book: _EXPERIENCE POEMS AND PICTURES_: _Poetry that Paints/Pictures that Speak_ (2019) with the section Reflections in four languages: English, French, German, and Spanish. Here newest book for scholars teaching students in first-year college general education classes is <u>PLANNING WITH PURPOSE: A Handbook for New College Teachers.</u>

One of her favorite scriptures is: (Proverbs 3:5-6)

> *Trust in the LORD with all thine heart;*
> *and lean not unto thine own understanding.*
> *In all thy ways acknowledge him,*
> *and he shall direct thy paths.*

Contact Anna at: ajroseboro@gmail.com
http://teachingenglishlanguagearts.com/

Jacqueline Smith

Apostle, Jacqueline Smith (Jae') calls herself a nobody. She is ministering by the Spirit of God carrying the mantle of authority, with might, and power. As an intercessor, baring in travail, and anointing to birth out, walks in discerning spirits. Also, she operates in the gifts of administration and organization. Apostle Jacqueline Apostle was called at the age of 17 like Samuel 3 times as he did, she went to her father. Ten years later, she understood the call, capacity, and responsibility for her life.

In 2004, Apostle Jae' was ordained a Minister under the Leadership of the Late Bishop Eugene J. Steward of Greater Bethel Temple in Louisville. In 2014, she founded Anointed Women Empowered Ministry. In August 2016, she established Divine Revelations Ministries, which is NOW Fresh Oil Ministries. Since then, God changed the whole trajectory of her life, Ministry & Vision. Downloads began, as God lay on her heart, to start subsidiaries of the Ministries to reach out to women.

In August 2018, Apostle Jacqueline established the Every Woman Needs A Woman Prayer Line & Facebook Group, Online Prayer, Prophecy & Preaching, an AWE extension. Also, she has developed a team of ministers who are now ready to pray for others every day. In The Global International Watchmen and she holds' a 24-hour prayer every last Saturday of the month.

She became an author releasing her first book, Woman Of Strength, "Developing Powerful Fruit" on August 15th, 2020.

Apostle Jacqueline has a Mandate and an assignment to preach, teach, prophetically train, and equip the body of Christ through The word of God, by His Love, Grace, and Mercy. She reaches out to the lost, the abused, the addicted, and the wounded warriors on the front lines, those who have been discouraged, shutdown, & rejected, the castaways & those who nearly died striving to help themselves understand themselves.

One of her favorite scriptures is, (Luke 12:48)

But he that knew not, and did commit things worthy of stripes, shall be beaten with few stripes.
For unto whomsoever much is given,
of him shall be much required:
and to whom men have committed much,
of him they will ask the more.

Annette West

Annette West is a Holistic Wellness Life Coach, Author and Professor, publisher and book writing coach. She uses her gifted, anointed and appointed voice to minister and serve Christ and others. She has been married to John for 36 years and they have 3 adult children and 7 grandchildren.

For over 35 years, it has been her goal to find ways to better care for her mind, body, and spiritual walk. As she grows, sharing and empowering others, growth is always her goal. She believes that when we learn to maintain an optimal level of wellness, we are aligned better with God and His expectation for our lives.

Annette has degrees in Business Administration, Management, Human Resources, and Pastoral Counseling, and is certified as a Pastoral Counselor and Holistic Wellness Coach and Master Life Coach.

She has traveled to many countries as a gospel vocalist and praise leader, orating God's truth. She has presented leadership training and various other topics for all genders and age groups. She helped start and continues to sponsor a mission school in Kakamega, E. Africa. She was one of the weekly voices on Life Conversations, PowerandPraiseRadio, and the voice on Living Holistically Well Podcast.

One of her favorite scriptures is, (James 1:22)

But be ye doers of the word,
and not hearers only,
deceiving your own selves.

Website: Drannettewestministries.org
 JATNEpublishing.org

Yolanda Whitehead

Yolanda Whitehead is a native of upstate New York. She is married to Terrance, an Air Force Veteran, and together they raise their two children in South Carolina. Yolanda has earned a bachelor's degree in Business Administration and a master's in Human Resources Development. Aside from being a full-time wife and mother, she works as a Benefits Specialist within her local school district. Yolanda enjoys the Human Resources field because it provides an opportunity to help others.

Over the last six years, Yolanda's life experiences challenged and at the same time transformed her into the woman of God that she is today. She doesn't push the word; she introduces the gospel to those around her in a way that they want to hear more. She has served within the church in the children's ministry and a small group leader in the sisterhood ministry. She has recently become comfortable sharing her life testimonies, hoping they can encourage belief within those who may experience their own trials.

One of her favorite Bible verses is (Romans 12:2,)

Do not conform to the pattern of this world,
but be transformed by the renewing of your mind.
Then you will be able to test and
approve what God's will is –
his good, pleasing and perfect will."

Robin Denise Whitehead-Rudolph

Robin Denise Whitehead-Rudolph is a mother and grandmother. She is also an ordained minister, a music director, church schoolteacher, lyricist, playwright, military veteran, and singer. She is also the owner of "Created For Me By You," a platform for spiritual writings including plays and training for religious education and photography.

She has a master's degree in Performance Improvement, Bachelors in Business Management, Associate degrees in Education and Business Management, and several certificates in religious studies. Robin has also written several booklets for Christian growth and maturity and often serves as a guest speaker at conferences.

During her time in the military, Robin worked as a representative to support equal opportunity. She focused on suicide intervention issues, victim advocate groups, rape crisis, and various youth and women programs in Germany, Georgia, Guam, Hawaii, New Jersey, New York, Oklahoma, Pennsylvania, and South Carolina. Robin is a United States Army retiree and lives in Ruther Glen, Virginia, where she has established Delicate Love and Nothing But The Truth Ministries.

One of her favorite scriptures is (Romans 8:28),

And we know that all things work together
for good to them that love God,
to them who are the called
according to his purpose.

Scriptures for Further Study
King James Version "KJV" Bible

The below scriptures are beyond the ones shared in each devotion. More scriptures to empower!

PSALM 28:7

The LORD is my strength and my shield; my heart trusted in him, and I am helped: therefore my heart greatly rejoiceth; and with my song will I praise him.

PROVERBS 3:5–6

Trust in the LORD with all thine heart; and lean not unto thine own understanding. In all thy ways acknowledge him, and he shall direct thy paths.

MATTHEW 6:33

But seek ye first the kingdom of God, and his righteousness; and all these things shall be added unto you.

ROMANS 8:28

And we know that all things work together for good to them that love God, to them who are the called according to his purpose.

ROMANS 8:38–39

For I am persuaded, that neither death, nor life, nor angels, nor principalities, nor powers, nor things present, nor things to come, Nor height, nor depth, nor any other creature, shall be able to separate us from the love of God, which is in Christ Jesus our Lord.

ROMANS 10:10

For with the heart man believeth unto righteousness; and with the mouth confession is made unto salvation.

ROMANS 12:2

And be not conformed to this world: but be ye transformed by the renewing of your mind, that ye may prove what is that good, and acceptable, and perfect, will of God.

1 CORINTHIANS 11:1–2

Be ye followers of me, even as I also am of Christ. Now I praise you, brethren, that ye remember me in all things, and keep the ordinances, as I delivered them to you.

GALATIANS 2:20

I am crucified with Christ: nevertheless I live; yet not I, but Christ liveth in me: and the life which I now live in the flesh I live by the faith of the Son of God, who loved me, and gave himself for me.

PHILIPPIANS 4:13

I can do all things through Christ who strengthens me.

PHILIPPIANS 1:20–21

According to my earnest expectation and my hope, that in nothing I shall be ashamed, but that with all boldness, as always, so now also Christ shall be magnified in my body, whether it be by life, or by death. For to me to live is Christ, and to die is gain.

JAMES 4:2–4

Ye lust, and have not: ye kill, and desire to have, and cannot obtain: ye fight and war, yet ye have not, because ye ask not. Ye ask, and receive not, because ye ask amiss, that ye may consume it upon your lusts. Ye adulterers and adulteresses, know ye not that the friendship of the world is enmity with God? whosoever therefore will be a friend of the world is the enemy of God.

ROMANS 6:3–4

Know ye not, that so many of us as were baptized into Jesus Christ were baptized into his death? Therefore we are buried with him by baptism into death: that like as Christ was raised up from the dead by the glory of the Father, even so we also should walk in newness of life.

ROMANS 12:1

I beseech you therefore, brethren, by the mercies of God, that ye present your bodies a living sacrifice, holy, acceptable unto God, which is your reasonable service.

COLOSSIANS 3:1

If ye then be risen with Christ, seek those things which are above, where Christ sitteth on the right hand of God.

Other Books by Dr. Annette West

Living Words of Encouragement Vol 1

Living Words of Encouragement Vol 2

The Book of Isaiah: 23-Day Devotional

Jesus the Path to Victorious Living

Holistic Wellness Mind Body Spirit

Holistic Wellness Mind Body Spirit (journal)

Basic Biblical Building Blocks Booklet

Entrepreneurship: Making Money God's Way in God's Time

New book release February 2021

Marriage Connection…making it work

Interested in writing your book reach out to me.

Contact Dr. Annette West at

JATNEpublishing@mail.com

If you enjoyed this book, please go to Amazon.com, select this book title, below author name you will see stars. Please leave a 5-star review and comment sharing what you liked about the book, how it helped you and recommend it to others.
Thank you in advance.

This source is: Spiritual -- Christian -- Daily Living – Devotional -- Bible Study -- Teaching Source – Counseling Source -- Empowerment

www.ingramcontent.com/pod-product-compliance
Lightning Source LLC
Chambersburg PA
CBHW071839090426
42737CB00012B/2294